DEATH

Through the Eyes of a
Funeral Director

DEATH

Through the Eyes of a Funeral Director

William Ellenberg

ومومو

Anneewakee River Press
Douglasville, Georgia

Published by Anneewakee River Press
P.O. Box 456, Douglasville, Georgia 30133-0456

The paper in this book meets the guidelines for
permanence and durability of the Committee on
Production Guidelines for Book Longevity of the
Council on Library Resources.

Library of Congress Catalog Card Number:

Printed in the United States of America

99 98 97   6 5 4 3 2 1

*This book is dedicated
to the memory of
Timothy Maddox*

June 21, 1963 — March 30, 1980

Introduction

Why You Need This Book

One of the lessons my twenty years as a funeral director has taught me is that I am often the person people <u>least</u> want to see or talk to. There is no need for them to explain. I know that the very idea of death and funerals makes them uncomfortable.

It should not be this way. A funeral director is the one person everyone will eventually need to meet, talk to, and work with. A funeral director is, among other things, an advocate for members of the grieving family, carrying out their wishes and handling logistical arrangements for them.

It is unfortunate the funeral home has been portrayed in film and on television as a foreboding, cold, scary place. It is intended to be a place of order and comfort.

I consider my chosen profession to be a high calling, one of ultimate service and commitment to the community. You may not perceive the managers and staff of your local funeral homes in this way and you would not be alone.

As people begin to understand what funeral directors actually do, the myths associated with funeral homes, embalming, and burial procedures would be dispelled. I sincerely believe perceptions would change if people knew the depths of empathy, the commitment of reliability, and the significant amount of difficulty involved in helping families say good-bye to their loved ones.

In this book, names have been changed to protect the privacy of the bereaved. Also, each section will end with questions. I encourage you to review them and if at all possible discuss them with your loved ones. There are blank pages for you to record your thoughts on the subject. At the end of this book I've included a glossary of terms.

It is my hope this book will help you become more familiar with and less frightened of the services funeral homes offer for these are services all of us will someday need.

William Ellenberger, III

Family Discussion

1. How comfortable or uncomfortable do you feel in the presence of a funeral director? Why?

Just be close to a funeral home make me very uncomfortable. it just do.

2. How would you feel living next door to a funeral home? Why?

Wouldn't like to living next door to one
I sure not be uncomfortable about living
Next door

3. What personality traits do you feel a funeral director should have? Discuss.

Help you put your love one away

4. Do you feel you and your family discuss the issue of death and dying too much or too little?

WE don't discuss the issue of death
it ALL

"If you need me, feel free to call me. If you need me to come out to your house right now and bring chairs or something like that — if you need anything at all, let me know. I will be glad to help you with whatever you need."

1

The Telephone Call

I had just returned from a five-day trade conference upstate. It was two a.m. on a Saturday. The neighborhood was peaceful as I rounded the corner of my street and pulled into the driveway. I walked in the door, weary and intending to go right to sleep. The telephone was ringing.

Before I picked up the receiver, I knew what the call would be — another family was in crisis and needed my help.

This time the call was from a nurse manager at Rosewood, a local convalescent home. Mr. John Evans, Sr., an elderly man, had just died in his sleep, she explained, and his family requested the services of the funeral home where I was the director.

I put my suitcase down and quickly got a pencil and notepad. I wrote down the important details I would need, most importantly the name and telephone number of Mr. Evans' next of kin.

There would be little if any sleep for me as the night progressed. This is normal for a funeral director. Our work day begins at any hour of the night when someone makes that first call.

Sometimes, the call will come from the emergency room just after the team of physicians and nurses have taken off their gear, turned off the equipment, and walked away from the operating table.

Sometimes, the call comes from the scene of an accident and over the phone I can hear the sounds of passing traffic in the background. To the passengers in those cars it is just another accident scene they see as they drive by. To the family of those killed in the accident, the world has stopped turning.

Whatever the origin of the call, whatever the time of day or night, I stop what I am doing or postpone what I had been planning to do and give my full attention to the family who has requested my help. The needs of that family and the loss of their loved one will probably be on my mind constantly from the time my telephone rings until days after the funeral itself. Their issues, their concerns, their priorities become mine as well.

It is a twenty-four hour day, three hundred and sixty five days a year commitment.

~ ~ ~ ~ ~

After I receive the initial call the next step is to telephone the family member named as the next of kin. This is the person the family has chosen to work with me as we make funeral arrangements.

One may think that because I make this kind of call several times a week, it is easy and automatic for me to discuss the funeral and the facts of the person's death with the grieving family members. It is probably just a casual conversation for me, right?

Wrong!

If anything, having that conversation so many times has made me more sensitive to the loss the family is facing. As I dial the number, I am thinking about that family and their loved one.

Because every family is unique, no two conversations are exactly the same. Although I am not a psychologist, I know that families and individuals have different ways of dealing with grief. The person I speak with may be in a state of shock, may be very emotional and unable to carry on a conversation with me, or may be irritable, overwhelmed by all that must be done over the next few days.

When I called Mr. Evans' family, his son, John, Jr., answered the phone.

"This is William Ellenburg from the funeral home," I began. "The nurse manager at Rosewood just called me to inform me that Mr. Evans passed away."

"Yes. He died about two hours ago," he answered. His voice was low and formal.

"I'm sorry to have to call you tonight and I'm sorry to hear that Mr. Evans passed away," I said. "I understand this is a difficult time, but there are just a few questions I need to ask you."

I never know whether saying "I'm sorry" will be any comfort or will mean anything to the bereaved relative. Nonetheless, I always say it. I was honestly sorry that Mr. Evans had died and I wanted his son to know it. It was important that I acknowledge his father's death as a terrible loss and not as a business transaction.

This first conversation will always set the tone for my relationship with the family. It should never be handled flippantly or too hastily. This is especially true of the next question I had to ask.

"I am required by state law to ask you if it is all right to go ahead and embalm him. If that is what you want?"

"Sure. Yes, go ahead," he answered. "We want a traditional funeral."

This is not always the answer I will get.

The word 'embalm' seems to upset some people and I can understand why. Embalming is a process few understand. Many people do not want to think about it, much less talk about it.

Its purpose is actually very simple — to improve the loved one's appearance and thus help preserve a serene and pleasant memory for family and friends.

Some people can not bear the thought of anything being 'done' to their loved one. It is as if they think morticians haphazardly experiment on and therefore abuse the body of the person who has passed away. In truth, embalming is a science and is conducted with much care, precision, and strict attention to state regulations.

Of course, not everyone who says 'no' to embalming is afraid or misinformed. Some, for example, know their loved one wanted to be cremated. This is completely the family's choice and it is for this reason I am required by state law to ask, even though the subject is difficult to bring up and difficult for the relatives to hear.

Once Mr. Evans' son gave his answer, we scheduled a time later in the day for the family to meet with me at the funeral home to make definite arrangements.

Waiting several hours before making those arrangements is usually a good thing — for the funeral director and the family. I needed time to freshen up, rest or sleep for an hour or so, and get organized.

The family needed time to discuss options among themselves as well as insure that an appointment with me was on their list of the day's tasks.

Many times a grieving person lives from hour to hour or even from minute to minute, just going through the motions while feeling shocked and disoriented. Often it is the small routine things like choosing clothes for the funeral, picking up relatives at the airport, and even having an appointment with the funeral director that helps them get through the day.

Before we hung up, I told Mr. Evans' son one more thing.

"I am going to give you my home phone number. If you need me, feel free to call me. If you need me to come out to your house right now and bring chairs or something like that — if you need anything at all, let me know. I will be glad to help you with whatever you need."

This is not a polite statement I use to end the conversation gracefully. This is my expression of a sincere wish to be of service, to offer my professional expertise as well as a helping hand to the family to whom I am now committed.

One should expect this level of sensitivity and dedication from a funeral director beginning with the initial telephone call.

Family Discussion

1. Name the funeral directors and/or morticians you know socially. What personality traits do they have in common, if any?

2. If you and your family needed the services of a funeral home tomorrow, which one in your community would you select? Why?

3. Do you recall your own feelings of shock and sadness when you received news that a friend or loved one had died? Share your recollections.

4. What do you think it would be like to be on alert, to stop your routine and plan the funerals of strangers? Do you think you would become apathetic about death? Do you think you would become more sensitive to others' sorrow? Discuss.

I will <u>never</u> refer to someone's loved one as 'the body.' That person is someone's father or mother, brother or sister, wife, husband, or child and will be treated as such by me and every member of my staff.

2

Keeping in Touch

I quietly placed the telephone receiver in its cradle. The Evans family, as I recalled, had lived in this town for many years — the son may have been a few grades a head of me in school. Their house was near the park where I played as a child and I remembered they attended church in one of the old historic churches on the courthouse square.

They were not so very different from my own family, I mused as I switched on the kitchen lights. In fact, next time it could be one of my parents.

Eventually, it <u>would</u> be.

It was not time to relax or drift off to sleep. The next step was to look after and carry out the family's wishes concerning Mr. Evans himself.

Some funeral homes in urban areas have large staffs and would have two different sets of people serving the Evans family — one to oversee and conduct the embalming and one to coordinate the funeral and burial. In most towns, however, the funeral home staff is involved in every aspect of the services it provides. I, along with one of my associates, would go to Rosewood to look after Mr. Evans.

~ ~ ~ ~ ~

When we arrived at Rosewood, it was five o'clock in the morning. Our job would involve more than just retrieving Mr. Evans and taking him back to the funeral home. There would be papers to sign and procedures to follow.

This would be the case whether we were going to a nursing home, a hospital morgue, or a hospice. When our destination is a residence, we work in cooperation with the supervising physician or, if there is none, the county coroner. It is unlawful for us to remove a person from any premises unless that person has been officially pronounced dead by the physician or the coroner.

Whatever the circumstances, we must be prepared to follow proper procedure without any hesitation.

When my staff and I are entrusted with funeral arrangements we are taking responsibility for complying with every regulation as required by law. We scrupulously follow every procedure and we 'do it by the book'.

The Evans family should not worry about whether forms such as the 'body release' form and the 'personal effects' form have been completed. We do those things for them and bring copies of the signed forms back to the funeral home.

~ ~ ~ ~ ~

Taking Mr. Evans into our custody, we drove back to the funeral home.

Notice I say 'Mr. Evans' and not 'the body'. This is something I do on purpose. I feel strongly about it. As long as I am a funeral director, I will <u>never</u> refer to someone's loved one as 'the body.' That person is someone's father or mother, brother or sister, wife, husband, or child and will be treated as such by me and every member of my staff.

Once we arrived at the funeral home, my assistant took Mr. Evans to the embalming room. I still had one more telephone call to make. His family needed to know that we had him in our care and were proceeding to comply with their wishes. Did the Evans family need to be interrupted at 6 a.m.?

Yes. I consider it extremely important to keep the family informed as my staff and I serve

15

them. During such a difficult time, it is some comfort to know that we are at their service and are taking excellent care of their loved one.

"Thank you," John Evans, Jr. said before we hung up. "We really appreciate your promptness."

As for me, I put my personal plans on hold for the next three days. Though I would have liked to go home and get some sleep, I needed to supervise the embalming process, which had to be done with extreme care and precision.

Soon it would be time for the Evans family to meet with me to make detailed funeral plans.

Family Discussion

1. How large a staff do you think a funeral home should have?

2. Before reading this chapter, how and by whom did you think people who have just died were removed from hospitals or nursing homes?

3. When members of a funeral home staff go to make a removal, why is it important for them to follow certain rules of etiquette in order to avoid being insensitive to others on the premises?

NOTES

1. SIX OR MORE

I can not emphasize enough how much easier the planning process is on the family members when they are in one accord on the best way to honor their loved one.

3

Planning the Funeral

I was straightening some papers on my desk when the secretary called me to let me know the Evans family had arrived for the three o'clock appointment.

By now, both the family and members of my staff had been up all night and I knew I was in need of some sleep, myself, in order to be at my best. That is the way it works sometimes — the part of my job that requires the most composure and sensitivity comes when I am operating on very little sleep and when I have a long list of other important items to attend to. Serving the family, however, must remain my top priority.

Working with families is not like following a step-by-step procedure that is always done a certain way with the same results every time. Families are complex systems composed of thinking, feeling individuals. Families have traditions and customs unique to them, traditions they cherish and want to see conducted as part of the funeral arrangements.

I have found that the more respect I give these customs, the more at peace the family seems to be throughout the planning process.

I reminded myself of all this as I walked out to the lobby to greet the Evans family. The son, John Evans, Jr., was there along with his sisters, Barbara and Marie, and their mother, John, Sr.'s wife, Alice. They all looked tired and a bit disoriented and I quickly felt my own discomfort replaced by a wave of compassion. They were depending on me and the funeral home to show them the way through a very difficult and unfamiliar maze of choices.

We walked back to my office and took our seats. There were so many things to be decided — date and time of the funeral, obituary content, type of funeral, type of coffin, preferences about the burial, and much more. I was coordinating all of it, so it was up to me to start the conversation.

"Have you thought about a day and time for the funeral?"

This is always a good place to begin, as the family is likely to be in agreement.

I can not emphasize enough how much easier the planning process is on the family members when they are in one accord on the best way to honor their loved one. Disagreements, jealousies, power struggles, and grudges have a tendency to show themselves during the planning session. Such disagreement, I have observed, come at great pain to the other members of the family and make it difficult for me to do my job.

~ ~ ~ ~ ~

With the Evans family, the discussion started out smoothly.

"We were thinking that the day after tomorrow would be the best day since Dad's brother won't arrive until tomorrow afternoon," John, Jr., said. "Could we have the service mid-morning?"

Some funeral homes have several chapels and are able to schedule multiple funerals during any given morning or afternoon. This particular facility had only one chapel but my calendar showed Monday morning was open.

We decided on an 11 a.m. funeral with burial following in the family plot in a cemetery on the outskirts of town.

By law, I am required to take information from the family in order to complete and file the death certificate. I also need to know some biographical facts to write an obituary for the local paper.

So, I listened and took notes as Alice Evans told me about her husband — first, the statistics such as his Social Security number, his height and weight for the death certificate, then the more personal facts for the obituary.

As she spoke, sometimes interrupted by her children as they added details and interesting facts, Alice told the story of her husband's life.

He was born in Philadelphia in 1922 and moved here after World War II when he was honorably discharged as a master sergeant in the US Army. He had been president of the Lions Club, a deacon in the church, a Cub Scout Pack leader, and manager of a local car dealership for more than twenty years.

This was the type of information I needed to know in order to plan the best and most meaningful funeral service for the family. The family, of course, would choose the pallbearers, the special music to be played, the scripture to be read, and the people who would speak during the program. The family would also choose the minister or another person they wanted to officiate at the service.

It was my responsibility to make certain everything came together gracefully. I wanted those who attended the funeral to feel they had witnessed a fitting tribute to someone they held in high esteem.

As I listened to the family talk about John Evans' life, I began to get a sense of the man he was, what was important to him and what his dreams were. The better I understood, the better the job I would do in directing the funeral.

I also noticed that talking about John's life seemed to encourage rather than upset his family. This is usually the case with almost all of the families during the funeral conference.

Another reason for me to listen very carefully is to make sure I record all the facts correctly. Seeing an obituary published is very important to family members. The announcement represents the loved one and what his or her life had been about.

~~~~~

As for the death certificate, the funeral director is required by law to record accurate information for prompt delivery to the county courthouse. The funeral director is responsible both to the family and to the state for seeing that this is done and done properly.

We talked about the actual events the funeral home would be hosting. The Evans family had already established that they wanted John, Sr. to have a traditional funeral in the funeral home chapel instead of the church sanctuary. They did, however, have any number of options.

First, they could have selected a family-only graveside service without any viewing of their loved one. This preference would not have required embalming, since the whole purpose of embalming is to enhance the person's appearance. This option would also not require the purchase of a traditional casket, which is usually the most expensive part of the cost of funeral services.

Second, they might have chosen to have a private viewing followed by a graveside service or memorial service.

When a family selects a private viewing only, they reserve for themselves the opportunity to see their loved one as opposed to allowing all their friends and family to see him or her in the setting of a pre-funeral visitation.

They could request a memorial service rather than a funeral. At most funerals, the loved one has been embalmed and is there in either a closed or open coffin for the benefit of all who have gathered to say good-bye.

Memorial services, on the other hand, are generally conducted without the presence of the coffin and are sometimes conducted in cities far from where the actual burial will take place. Mrs. Evans, for example, might have wanted a memorial service held in Philadelphia where she and her husband grew up, met, married, and had many friends and relatives.

They had another option. Cremation.

It is unusual for the family to request that their loved one be cremated unless he or she had specifically stated it or had put it in writing that this was the preference. More and more people are requesting cremation, however, and it is gaining acceptance in our culture as a respectable alternative.

If Mr. Evans had specified cremation as his preference, his family could have decided to purchase a specially made urn for his ashes from the funeral home or buy some other appropriate container elsewhere. The funeral home could also have arranged for the container to be buried in a local cemetery.

The funeral director should always provide the family with a comprehensive price list outlining all the alternatives and the price of each. The cost for these services will vary according to which combinations are selected. The director will gladly organize and host the type of service the family wants.

Alice Evans and her children wanted a visitation night for family and friends in addition to the traditional funeral. The morticians would do their professional best to insure Mr. Evans looked serene and at peace. While I was meeting with the Evans family, they were already at work to ready him for the visitation the next night.

There was still one more major decision to be made: the choice of a casket.

Family Discussion

1. How often do you read the obituaries in your local newspaper? Do you consider them an important part of the day's news? How so?

2. How do you feel about cremation as an option for your own funeral arrangements?

3. What can be done in advance to help prevent family squabbling during the conference with the funeral director?

NOTES

Sometimes what they need is privacy.

4

Selecting the Casket

I led the members of the Evans family out of my office and down the hall to the casket room, a gallery where the funeral home displays representative types of caskets available to families.

John Evans, Jr. narrowed his eyes and looked at me suspiciously. I had just given each family member a price list printed on a sheet of paper. I could tell he thought I was trying to cheat him.

I know that there are unethical funeral directors out there who will try to influence bereaved families to spend as much money as possible on the funeral, coffin, and burial. It is true that these items can be quite expensive — too expensive for the average family. Many funeral directors, however, are genuinely concerned about the needs of the family and not about the size of his or her personal bank account.

I had no interest in seeing how much money the funeral home could get from the Evans family.

My concern was that the funeral home provide the best quality coffin in a price range with which they would be comfortable.

It is true that caskets can be the single most expensive item on the funeral bill. The price range, however, is broad with units available from about $300 to over $5,000.

The question was simply this: what would John, Sr. have wanted and what did the family think was appropriate?

"I think he would have wanted a plain pine box," answered Barbara, with conviction. "He wouldn't want anything fancy."

This was certainly an option. Many people do have a preference for a wooden casket, sometimes for the natural simplicity it offers and sometimes because it is more economical. Not all wooden caskets are alike. It is possible to choose from hardwood, softwood, plywood as well as finished wood or cloth-covered wood.

Caskets that are made of metal will be more expensive than those made of wood. They are also more protective. Usually made of copper, steel or bronze, these caskets are designed for strength and durability. Many metal caskets will have a protective sealer to help keep out moisture and prevent rust. These caskets are often purchased with a warranty. This warranty, however, is not a guarantee that moisture will not penetrate the unit.

"You should know that the Federal Trade Commission prohibits me or any other funeral director from making claims that certain caskets can ensure perpetual preservation," I told the John Evans' family with complete frankness. No casket can do that."

John, Jr. relaxed a little and leaned back in his chair.

"And you should also know that you are not required to buy a casket with a sealer. No casket can keep every bit of the elements out, forever. A sealer just delays the inevitable."

Each family member had a copy of the price list. The last thing I wanted to do was make them feel pressured into buying something they did not think was appropriate for John, Sr. I designed the list to show families all of their options, not just the more expensive ones. The inexpensive caskets were presented in a manner just as dignified as those at the top of the price scale.

The Evans family could choose from a long list of alternatives — type of material, color, size, interior, etc. Explaining all their options to them was the easy part. The hard part, unfortunately, would turn out to be getting them to agree among themselves.

Alice and Marie favored choosing a medium-priced steel model. Barbara could not be persuaded that her father would want anything other than a plain pine box. John, Jr. wanted a bronze model with sealer and handles. It was clear the family had not reached an agreement on this with their father before his death.

Ideally, John, Sr. would have told his wife and children what he wanted and would have put his wishes in writing. He could have also paid for most of his funeral services in advance, simplifying the process for his family later.

At any rate, none of us had any way to verify that John Evans, Sr. wanted a pine casket. Barbara was outnumbered. She began to get very defensive and upset, insisting she alone was carrying out her father's wishes. John, Jr. was adamant that his father would want a metal casket that was highly durable. Alice was upset that her children were upset. Marie was annoyed with them all.

I have seen families get into shouting matches with each other over less. What happens, I think, is that the death of their loved one adds more stress to the relationships. People are tired, shocked, sad, angry, and irritable.

It does not take much conflict to flare tempers. In addition, I think they tend to be very sensitive about honoring the wishes of the person who has passed away. I have seen family members clash over everything from an affordable price range to color of the casket's interior.

~ ~ ~ ~ ~

I am not a family therapist. I do try, however, to help the family calm down and reach some sort of consensus.

Sometimes what they need is privacy.

"I'm going to leave the room for a few minutes," I told them. "Please try to get this worked out. I didn't know your father well, but I don't think he would be pleased to see you arguing like this."

While they were alone, Alice Evans was able to get the others to agree that she should have the final say. She pointed out that her husband was a practical man who valued moderation in everything he did. The steel casket fit that description.

John, Jr. still wanted a model with sealer, so Alice agreed to include that. In deference to her mother, Barbara stopped insisting on the pine casket, although she still felt she was right. Marie was ready to go home.

One more decision was still needed, however. The cemetery where Mr. Evans would be buried required every casket to be placed in either a burial vault or a less expensive grave liner. I gave each of the family members another price list so they could choose. Happily, they agreed right away that they wanted a burial vault, made of concrete reinforced with steel, instead of the grave liner.

The total cost of the casket and burial vault came to $2800, an amount the family could comfortably afford. Although their discord and lack of consensus caused a few tense moments, I was pleased, overall, with the service I had given them up to that point.

If I had done my job ethically and properly, John Evans, Jr. would revise his opinion of funeral directors as greedy salespeople.

Family Discussion

1. Do you think caskets are over priced? Why or why not?

2. Compare the cost of a funeral with the cost of a wedding. Which should be more expensive?

3. What type of casket do you think you would want for yourself? Have you discussed this with members of your family?

NOTES

What I do is constantly remind myself that death, although irreversible and inevitable, is a natural process.

5

The Facts About Embalming

After the meeting with the Evans family, I went to the mortuary to check on the progress of the mortician and his apprentice. Their task was of the utmost importance. Within twenty-four hours, several hundred people would view Mr. Evans at the visitation. If he did not look natural, the way his friends and loved ones remembered him, the funeral home would have failed in its effort to provide them with one final pleasant memory of him.

That is what embalming really is all about. It is, I think, probably the most prominent part of the entire funeral home myth. Many people are convinced that embalming is a 'creepy' process conducted by a weirdo who gets a thrill from manipulating corpses.

On the contrary, embalming is both a scientific and a cosmetic procedure governed by strict regulations and conducted with much care.

Professional morticians attend a special school where they are taught the proper and exact procedure for embalming as well as the history and purposes of the embalming. They are also taught the psychology and sociology of death and the funeral process, enabling them to be as sensitive as possible to the fears and misunderstandings people have.

I attended school in Atlanta where I studied the science of embalming much in the same way a medical student studies surgery. I also studied the art of embalming, much in the same way an art student studies color and form. As a Licensed Funeral Director, I was required to pass a State Board licensing examination and complete a year-long apprenticeship working under the supervision of experienced professionals.

Let me share with you a few things I have learned about why and how the deceased are embalmed.

Embalming as an art and a science began in ancient Egypt when death was considered a temporary separation of body and spirit. The Egyptians believed the spirit would, after several thousand years, eventually return to earth in search of its body. For this reason they considered it very important to keep the body in good condition.

There was also a practical reason behind the ancient Egyptian tradition: sanitation. A series of catastrophic floods caused large numbers of deaths at one time in Egypt. The ground was so saturated with water the dead could not be buried. Embalming was a solution to this problem.

The Egyptians' tradition was not necessarily adopted by other cultures. The religious traditions of the Jews, the early Christians, and the people of the Roman Empire dictated different burial customs. None of these groups saw the need to preserve the body for extended lengths of time.

It was not until the Medieval period in Europe that embalming again became a common procedure but usually for the purpose of preserving cadavers for medical experimentation. The Roman Catholic Christianity practiced by most of Europe taught that the soul, freed by death, had no need of its body once it entered the supernatural realm. Embalming had no religious basis or spiritual importance during that time.

Over time scientific interest in human physiology increased. Embalming remained an essential practice as medical knowledge grew. In the early years of the 18th century, a Dutch anatomy professor named Dr. Frederick Ruysch pioneered the practice of arterial injection as a means of preserving a deceased body. Prior to his research, embalming methods were primitive using less gentle and more invasive methods.

Up until the time of the American Civil War, embalming was a routine practice for medical research. Occasionally it was performed for funerals at a family's request. Sometimes members of European royal families were embalmed so their bodies could be displayed before their interment. This was a luxury exclusively for the elite.

The Civil Way changed everything. Thousands of soldiers were dying great distances from home. Doctors had to find a way to preserve their bodies for the long trips from the battlefields in the South to New England townships. Dr. Thomas Holmes, commonly called the "Father of Modern Embalming in the United States", embalmed a number of Union officers who were killed in combat.

Before the end of the war, Dr. Holmes opened his own mortuary in Washington, D.C. and made his services available to families of more than 4,000 soldiers. Working people — not just the aristocrats — wanted the bodies of their loved ones preserved for a while before burial.

Nonetheless, actual arterial injection was rarely used by undertakers. It was primarily a scientific research practice. Instead, morticians would just pack the body of the deceased in crushed ice — an easy method of short-term preservation. This method, however, was too temporary, especially if the body had to be shipped or transported from one part of the country to another.

~ ~ ~ ~ ~

In the latter half of the 19th century, doctors were able to simplify the embalming-by-injection process. The average undertaker could safely and successfully perform the procedure. Soon it was possible for the body of a loved one to look very natural days after death, no matter what the climate. This was a revolution in the funeral industry as well as in the American culture.

More families wanted their deceased loved ones embalmed. More morticians were needed. Soon there were licensing requirements designed to enforce high standards and competence in the profession.

Embalming continues to be the standard in funeral preparations today.

I think it is interesting to note that, unlike the ancient Egyptians, its acceptance and normality has nothing to do with religion.

Religious and non-religious people alike choose to have their deceased relatives embalmed. The practice is compatible with the Judeo-Christian tradition as well as with the other major religions practiced in the United States.

~ ~ ~ ~

The best way I know to help people understand what actually happens in the embalming room is to explain what we do, step by step. Although it is true I never refer to a person's loved one as 'the body' when I am talking to a family member, I am going to use this term now as I explain how embalming is done. I will not be talking about any actual person.

First, we bring the body in from the funeral coach to the preparation room and place it on a large table, similar to what is used in hospitals when doctors conduct autopsies. I want it understood that it is here where the similarity between an autopsy and embalming end. Forensic pathologists conduct autopsies. Medical students conduct dissections. Morticians, however, are actually caring for the body — not exploring it, not taking it apart.

Next, we remove all of the clothing so we can clean the body. We either fold the clothing and return them to the family or we destroy them.

The standard method of cleaning is with a disinfectant spray or disinfectant solution. This process is extremely important to reduce the risk of contagious disease. Although the body is no longer a live, the germs it may be carrying are and have the potential to infect the mortician and anyone else in the room.

My staff and I wear rubber gloves and special protective suits to shield us from communicable diseases such as tuberculosis. By order of OSHA (Occupational Safety and Health Administration), preparation rooms must have a first aid station in the event of chemical spills or injuries from the instruments.

A competent mortician will always follow, to the letter, all OSHA regulations and embalming procedures.

Once the disinfection is complete, we always cover the body with a sheet from the shoulders down. I believe every person, living or dead, deserves to be treated with dignity and respect. Making sure the private areas of the body are covered during the embalming is something I require all morticians and apprentices under my supervision to do.

We keep the preparation room strictly off limits during an embalming. No one but the morticians, themselves, or possibly the coroner are authorized to see the body.

There is another standard all ethical morticians practice. They do not discuss what they see and do regarding a particular deceased person outside of the preparation room. This is an absolute requirement which I think is a matter of professionalism, morality, and trust.

After the body is covered, we position it the way we believe looks most natural. What we want and what the family usually wants is for the person to appear to be sleeping. In order to accomplish this, we must preserve the appearance of sleep. We do this by arterial injection.

Arterial injection is the process where we make two small incisions, one over an artery and one over a vein. We connect an intravenous (IV) type apparatus to a special embalming instrument that provides the pressure required to circulate the fluid.

We aspirate — release the fluid or gases — from the abdominal or chest cavities via tubes and suction. We do not dissect the bodies or remove organs. We simply relieve pressure on the chest or abdomen through this process of aspiration.

Cosmetic specialists do the rest by completing what we call a 'memory picture', an image of the loved one that looks peaceful and natural.

This, of course, is a very simplified description of the embalming procedure. It is neither scary, creepy or gory. The rumors of bodies sitting up or of deceased people sneezing while on the embalming table are all untrue.

The preparation room of a funeral home is exceedingly clean, sanitary, and organized. Bodies of those who have passed away are treated with reverence and handled with extreme care.

~ ~ ~ ~ ~

Although extremely clinical, the process is not routine. Morticians generally handle each person as if he or she was their own parent or child. I have conducted and supervised many embalmings. I still find that I care very much about the 'memory picture' being created.

I remember the time I was entrusted with making a 'memory picture' of an infant boy who had died of Sudden Infant Death Syndrome (SIDS). I am not ashamed to tell you that I wept throughout the entire process. I imagined him as my own. I handled him gently and with great care. Even though I could not comprehend the depth of his parents' sorrow, I could express my empathy and concern through the creation of the 'memory picture'.

At times I am asked if it is emotionally difficult to embalm and prepare bodies. My answer is both, yes and no. Yes, I am sometimes affected by the circumstances of the death, as when I saw the profound grief the baby's parents were suffering. I do not try to block out the sadness of death, even though I am confronted with it every day. What I do is constantly remind myself that death, although irreversible and inevitable, is a natural process. It is natural that the body, once its life has ended, should 'return to the earth' — become one with the earth, enriching it.

When I was a child, I would bury the bodies of little animals — fallen birds, especially — unafraid to see that they were dead and that this was a natural part of a larger cycle. I always saw a certain dignity and beauty there.

Embalming delays the progress of that cycle a short while — long enough for those who love the deceased person to spend a few final moments with him or her.

A personal note: Does the subject of embalming still make you uncomfortable? If it does, I encourage you to try to talk about your concerns with a friend or family members, or perhaps even a funeral director you know and trust. When the time comes for you to be involved in planning a funeral for someone close to you, I believe you will find the process so much easier if you fully understand the procedure, itself, as well as all the services available to you.

Family Discussion

1. Based on what you have read in this chapter about the embalming process, what misconceptions did you have that are now corrected?

2. How would you feel about touring a funeral home, including the embalming facility?

3. What skills does a mortician need in order to perform an embalming properly and carefully?

Suddenly their gratitude for a job well done and their grief for the lost of the anchor of their family overwhelmed me.

6

The Visitation

By the time Sunday evening arrived, I had finally gotten eight hours of sleep and I was well prepared to host the visitation for Mr. Evans.

It was my responsibility to make sure that everything would be exactly as the family had requested: the dressing of Mr. Evans in the in the clothes they brought for him, placing him in the casket they selected, the arrangements of flowers in the visitation parlor, the rocking chairs set up on the front porch.

The visitation parlor itself looked hospitable and comfortable, not overly formal with an imposing decor. I think that funeral homes should first be soothing and comfortable, with stateliness and luxuriousness less important. People should feel almost as if they are in their own home receiving their closest friends and not in the lobby of an unfamiliar building.

The actual visitation was still two hours away. I sat down at my desk and read the morning paper. The first thing I looked for was Mr. Evans' obituary — the result of my rushing the information across town to the newspaper the day before.

Evans, John E.
John Edward Evans, 77, of 301 Weatherly St. died March 21, 1997, at Rosewood Convalescent Home after a long illness. He was born in Philadelphia, Pa., on June 7, 1920, the son of Terence and Jane (Allen) Evans. He was educated in the schools of Philadelphia. He served in the U.S. Army during World War II and received an honorable discharge as a master sergeant in 1946. He moved to Georgia in 1949 and worked at several car dealerships in town before becoming sales manager at Northside Chevrolet in 1959. He retired from Northside Chevrolet in 1983. Active in many civic clubs, he served as president of the Lions Club for two years and was a Cub Scout Pack leader for eight years. He is survived by a brother, Morris Evans of Philadelphia, Pa., a wife, Alice Hill Evans, three children: John Evans, Jr. of Atlanta, Marie Evans Tyler of Arlington, Va., and Barbara Evans Kelly of Tampa, Fla., and four grandchildren. Walton-Benefield Funeral Home is in charge of the arrangements. The family will be receiving friends and family Sunday

evening at 1 P.M. at the funeral home.
Funeral services are scheduled for 11
a.m. Monday in the chapel of the
funeral home. Memorial contributions
may be made to the Baptist Children's
Home.

Just below John Evans' obituary was an
obituary for someone named Annie Sue Gunther
who died one day after her one hundred and
fourth birthday. Below that was an obituary for a
21 year old man killed in a boating accident.

The thought that all of these people had
families who were grieving and who needed a
funeral director's services was almost
overwhelming. There were so many details to be
attended to, so many sensitivities.

Had I forgotten anything?

I opened my notebook and looked at the
checklist I had written out for the Evans'
arrangements. Everything appeared to be on
schedule. Mr. Evans had been embalmed. The
hairdresser and beautician had perfected his
appearance and had dressed him in the clothes
Alice Evans brought for him.

~ ~ ~ ~ ~

It was time for the family's private viewing.
This is the opportunity for the family and usually

only the adult members of the family, to see their loved one and spend some time with him or her in the privacy of the visitation parlor.

If the Evans family saw anything about Mr. Evans they wanted me to change or correct, there was ample time to do so.

Alice Evans and her three children arrived on time for the viewing. I escorted them into the flower-filled room. At first there was silence as they looked at Mr. Evans. Alice walked over to look more closely at her husband. John, Marie, and Barbara followed.

"He looks very nice," Alice whispered, her voice thick with suppressed emotion. "Thank you."

She turned to look at me. Her eyes were glowing with the wetness that would soon be tears. "Thank you."

To my surprise, I felt my own eyes begin to tear. I had stood in this exact place at private family viewings like this hundreds of times. Suddenly their gratitude for a job well done and their grief for the lost of the anchor of their family overwhelmed me. It was as if I was directing the first funeral of my career.

At seven o'clock friends of the family began to arrive. Car after car pulled into the parking lot. I watched as streams of people came through the front door. Some of them were former cub scouts who had known Mr. Evans as their Pack Leader. Some of them were Lions Club friends, young and old. Six of them would be pallbearers.

Some were childhood friends of his children who had read the obituary in the paper. They came to comfort them and renew acquaintances.

Whatever their relationship to the family, the people came to pay their respects to John Evans and to express sympathy to his wife, children, and grandchildren. Soon, the parlor was crowded and filled with sound as old friends embraced and shook hands.

~~~~~

Kristen Evans, John Jr.'s seven year old daughter, stood in the corner by the door, the farthest point in the room from the casket. She stared at her feet, the floor, the ceiling.

I had encouraged John, Jr., Barbara, and Marie to include their children in as many of the funeral and pre-funeral events as possible. The adults, however, had been concerned about whether the grandchildren, who ranged in age from four to sixteen, should attend the visitation and funeral.

My answer to that question is almost always 'yes'. Although children under the age of six do not fully comprehend what it means when a family member dies, they still have the same need for closure that adults have. They still have to have the chance to say good-bye and to realize that the loved one is actually no longer living.

Kristen was clearly uncomfortable. I suspected, however, that as the evening progressed she would be less so. Perhaps one of her older cousins or her parents would walk her over to see her grandfather. Maybe her parents would talk with her about her fears and her feelings later that night after the visitation.

Even though Kristen's confusion and discomfort would not magically go away as the result of any one conversation she might have, I was certain her attendance of the visitation and funeral would be an important part of her eventual understanding of death and of the healing process she would need.

Funerals and related events like visitations are actually very good for all those who are grieving. In some ways, the funeral is like a family reunion and can be a positive experience. It can be a celebration of the life and times of the person who has passed away. It can be a time of nurturing of the family relationships that will continue after the death.

Watching the people interact at the Evans visitation, I noticed they all either knew each other or were fast becoming acquainted. Alice Evans met the granddaughter of one of her husband's Lions Club friends. Marie introduced her best friend from high school to John, Jr.'s wife. The warmth in the room was almost tangible.

~ ~ ~ ~ ~

One phenomenon that occasionally presents a problem for me and for families is the unwelcome attendance of the curious at visitations and funerals.

The week before the Evans funeral, I was in charge of arrangements for a man who had died in a skydiving accident. His family was quite distressed and rightly so. A dozen or more thrill-seekers showed up at the visitation to see how he looked. They wanted to see what kind of embalming and cosmetic job we had done.

I suppose curiosity is normal in cases like that but it seems to me manners and respect are more important, a great deal more important.

In such instances, I will not hesitate to ask the curious to leave. I see it as an important part of my job. It is my responsibility to protect the

dignity of every family who has entrusted me
with funeral arrangements.

*A personal note: I encourage you to
include your children, depending on
their ages, in as many of the funeral
and pre-funeral events as possible.*

Family Discussion
**1. Have you ever attended a visitation at a funeral
home? What was the overall atmosphere like?
Was it warm or somber?**

**2. How did you feel about viewing the body of
the person who had died?**

**3. In what way is it more comfortable to receive
visitors than to spend the days prior to the funeral
in seclusion?**

NOTES

It is important to remember that grieving, whether quiet and private or expressive and public, is an appropriate part of the funeral.

7

The Funeral

My alarm went off at four o'clock Monday morning. I got out of bed and immediately began my pre-funeral agenda I had planned the night before — coffee and toast at four-thirty, shower at five. I planned to be in the office by six to prepare for the funeral at eleven.

Five hours working in and out of the office was not an unusually long block of time for a morning like this. There were flower arrangements to move, routes to the cemetery to check and double-check, limousine orders to confirm, and chairs to deliver to the Evans home for their friends and relatives who would gather informally after the burial.

By ten a.m., my staff and I had completed all these things and were ready to move on to a new list of tasks. The minister, Hugh Taylor, arrived. We discussed the order of the service and the content of the eulogy.

The minister was well-acquainted with the Evans family. Alice Evans called him, herself, immediately after her husband died.

Occasionally, a family will ask me to contact a Protestant minister, Roman Catholic priest, or Jewish rabbi for them so the funeral service will be conducted according to the appropriate religious tradition.

It is also common for families to request a nonreligious funeral service with or without our provision of someone to officiate. Whatever the family's wish, we can and will accommodate.

Pastor Taylor and I went over the program step by step. My staff and I would bring Mr. Evans in his casket into the chapel and place him in the traditional location, front and center near the podium. At the family's request, the casket would be closed during the service.

Prior to the actual service, while people were still entering the chapel and being seated, the organist would play several of Mr. Evans' favorite hymns.

I would then seat the family in a special area of the chapel where the others in attendance could not see them. We built our chapel with this type of seating arrangement in order to give the families privacy during such a highly emotional time. When funerals are conducted in church sanctuaries, the family usually sits together near the front in such a way for them to still have a measure of privacy.

Pastor Taylor would make his opening remarks and then several of Mr. Evans' friends would share their happiest memories of him. Alice's best friend, Myra Davis, would read one of his favorite poems. Pastor Taylor would then make a few additional remarks and read some selections from the Bible that Alice and the children had chosen.

The trend, I think, is moving away from just a eulogy and toward a more personal service which is usually dominated by the loving reminiscences of friends, the reading of poetry, and the singing of songs that had a personal significance to the deceased.

More and more funeral services are actually celebrations of the person's life — the highlights, the achievements, the things that brought happiness. I was glad the Evans family choose this type of service.

Whatever style is preferred, I recommend to families and officiants that they keep the service to about thirty minutes. Any less than that and people do not feel as if they have really had time to say good-bye. Any more than that and people start to get restless and the service becomes too emotionally difficult for some family members.

After Pastor Taylor concluded his remarks and invited everyone to the cemetery for the burial, I would give the pallbearers the signal to go forward and move the casket.

If all went smoothly, the service would happen exactly like that. I believe that planning and directing a funeral service is not any different from planning and directing a wedding. Both commemorate events in the life cycle of human beings. Both require a lot of detail work in order to make the ceremony seem effortless.

Once Pastor Taylor and I went over the parts of the service, it was time to send the limousines to pick up the Evans family. The rationale for this as a funeral tradition is that the family should not have to worry about their transportation or anything else in the days and hours leading up to the funeral.

~ ~ ~ ~ ~

At ten-forty people were beginning to arrive. My staff served as ushers to show them in to the chapel while I stayed with the family in a small room away from the entrance.

Little Kristen was wearing a beautiful pink cloud of a dress. She was silent and wide-eyed as she held her mother's hand. John, Jr. was somber and unusually quiet.

Alice Evans, who had previously kept her composure in our meetings and during the visitation, was starting to fall apart. I knew the service and burial would be particularly difficult for her. Over the past few days, I had noticed, the rest of the family had looked to her to set the tone, to tell them everything was all right.

I have seen grief sneak up on people like that, particularly when they have tried hard to be the 'rock' for everyone else. It is important to remember that grieving, whether quiet and private or expressive and public, is an appropriate part of the funeral. Tears are normal, even expected, and excessive emotional restraint is not a healthy way to cope with death.

Members of the Evans family were to be seated well out of sight of the other people. I hoped they would feel safe enough to release some of their grief.

An usher entered the room and gave the signal that it was time to bring the family into the chapel.

"We're all here this morning," Pastor Taylor began, "because of our love and respect for John Evans."

As far as I am concerned, there is no more appropriate opening statement. Some say funerals are not happy occasions, however, I see something positive and affirming in people gathering together to show their love and respect.

The minister continued with his eulogy, talking about John Evans' life and conversations on spiritual matters the two of them had in the months prior to his death.

Next, his close friend and former colleague from the car dealership, Gordy Schmidt, talked about some of the good times they shared as fishing buddies, as co-workers, as veterans, and as football enthusiasts.

Some of the anecdotes were light-hearted and humorous. People smiled and even chuckled softly at the story of how the two friends got lost during a fishing trip to North Carolina because both were too stubborn to ask for directions.

I think that humor can be entirely appropriate during funerals if it is done in a respectful and affectionate way. Outright jokes do not usually go over well but anecdotes designed to bring a smile are welcome.

"John Evans was a very perceptive man who listened a lot more than he talked," Mr. Schmidt shared. "He's still a legend at Northside Chevrolet for being the only salesman to recognize that a man dressed like a bum who the rest of us thought was just wandering around on our car lot was actually a man of means who intended to buy an expensive sedan on the spot. John treated him respectfully and took him seriously and the man paid cash for our top-of-the line model. But that was John...he could always tell when someone was sincere."

Other friends shared their favorite memories of John. Then, Myra Davis read a poignant and fitting poem about the joy of life and the greater joy ahead in the afterlife.

~ ~ ~ ~ ~

I moved from the back door of the chapel to the area where the Evans family were sitting. When it was time to exit the chapel and go to the cemetery, I would lead them out.

I could tell the service was meaningful to the family especially to John, Jr. who was smiling and nodding his head as he listened to the speakers talk about his father. Alice Evans, however, was struggling, occasionally smiling, alternately weeping, and trembling as she tried to keep her composure.

As Pastor Taylor made his closing remarks and said the closing prayer, I readied myself to escort the family out of the chapel and to the limousines. At my signal, John, Jr. stood up and the rest of the family followed.

All except Alice. She remained sitting, as if the drive to the cemetery would never come if she refused to acknowledge the service was over.

What could I do? It was my duty to do whatever I could to make things easier for her.

I leaned down and offered her my arm. No words were spoken. She took my arm and I helped her stand up. Then, still holding her up, I walked her out of the chapel myself and did not let go until she was safely in the limousine.

Do I do this at every funeral? No. It's a judgement call. I have to be sensitive to the family's needs. For some people, having the funeral director touch them for any reason would be out of the question. It would be an unwelcome intrusion.

With Alice Evans, however, something told me she needed my assistance and that it was all right to reach out to her.

Later, after the funeral and the burial, she told me how much she appreciated it.

"I just felt so safe and secure," she explained. "It made me feel that everything was under control."

As far as I am concerned, that sums up what being a funeral director is about.

Family Discussion

1. Have you ever been to a funeral you found uplifting and positive? Describe what you liked about it.

2. What do you think you would like your own funeral service to be like? What music would you select? Would you want friends to share their happiest memories of you? Who would you choose to officiate?

3. Have you ever attended a funeral that was emotionally difficult for you? What was your relationship to the person who had died? How did you cope with your grief?

There are some things about the cer-
emonies of death that are as poignant
and uplifting as the ceremonies of life.

8

Saying Good-bye

I helped Mrs. Evans into the limousine and shut the door tightly. The driver, a member of my staff, would see that she got to the cemetery safely and quickly. The other drivers of the limousines chaffering the rest of the family would do the same.

As for me, I also had to get to the cemetery right away. As director of the funeral, I would need to be there to see that traffic flowed smoothly on the route I had mapped the previous day. I would need to make certain the flower arrangements looked neat and attractive when the people arrived for the burial. And, I had to be sure the two rows of chairs for the Evans family were ready for them to use during the short graveside service.

Our purpose was to keep the Evans family from having to <u>think</u> about anything or worry about anything. The other people attending the burial should also not have to worry about where to park or where to stand.

This is a good example of why a funeral director needs to be much more than simply an embalmer. I have noted through out this book that a great deal of sensitivity is needed. Equally important is the ability to coordinate events and arrange logistical details.

When your car is just one in a long line of a caravan from the funeral home to the cemetery, you just follow the car in front of you and think little of the route. Your car turns into the driveway of the cemetery, as the driver winds through the green hills amid the grave markers and colorful wreaths of flowers. Think what would happen if the lead car went in the wrong entrance or took a wrong turn. Fifty or more cars would follow in confusion, in search of the correct green tent.

This is why by the time the Evans funeral procession turned left onto Main Street, the route had already been carefully rehearsed.

From the first time Alice Evans mentioned the name of the cemetery where her family owned a plot, we began planning for the graveside service and burial. Early in the morning before the funeral, in fact, I had visited the gravesite to help place the grass matting and to make sure the mechanism used to lower the casket into the grave was ready and operable.

Cemetery workers had been there early to open the grave. A worker from the burial vault company had also been there to install the vault.

The family had the option of having the casket lowered into the grave at the end of the burial service or having this done after all of the people had left. Feeling it was important for all those who loved and respected John Evans to see that he was laid to rest, they chose the first option.

If their plot had been in the city cemetery, we would have had to adhere to its rules. Such rules may be different from those required in the church cemetery. Some cemeteries require a headstone, at the very least, with many large monuments and mausoleums therefore being mixed in with smaller markers. Some cemeteries — often called 'memorial gardens' — do not allow stone markers and require bronze plaques instead.

If John Evans had wished to be buried in the veterans' cemetery in the next county, we would have complied with a different set of military regulations.

If they had owned a plot in another city, we would have led a procession there. The price — $100 — would have been the same within a 50-mile radius.

Many times, the family does not own a plot and one has to be purchased quickly.

Some, but not all, funeral homes also sell monuments. When the funeral home does not sell them, a staff member will handle the logistical details of the purchase for the family, based on their desired price range and other specifications.

~ ~ ~ ~ ~

Everything was ready for the Evans burial — the tent was up, the flowers were beautiful, the chairs were ready, and the cars were on their way. I could see them coming from a distance, moving down the hill toward the old brick church.

The funeral service and burial customs are sometimes called 'Homegoing Rites.' To me it seemed as if Mr. Evans was actually going home. Everywhere I looked in the cemetery, there were other Evans markers — his parents, grandparents, cousins, aunts, and uncle.

Pastor Taylor arrived followed by the three family limousines. I escorted the Evans family to the canopy at the gravesite where they could sit while their friends gathered around them.

The service was brief, but inspirational. Pastor Taylor read the verses I love from the New Testament. "I am the Resurrection and the Life. He who believes in me though he were dead, yet shall he live."

The week before I had directed a funeral officiated by a rabbi from the local Jewish synagogue. The words he read were in Hebrew and although I did not know what he said, they were, nonetheless, beautiful and soothing.

There are some things about the ceremonies of death that are as poignant and uplifting as the ceremonies of life.

"To everything there is a season," Pastor Taylor read, "and a time to every purpose under Heaven."

Those words were comforting and reassuring to me and I wondered about Alice Evans, her children and grandchildren.

The minister read the closing prayer. People began to line up to greet the John Evans family and to extend their condolences. For them, the funeral was over. They would return to their cars and resume their work day.

For the family, nothing was really over.

~ ~ ~ ~ ~

Attending and supervising burial services on at least a weekly basis, I have seen many different ways people cope with grief. John Evans' daughter, Barbara, was coping the way most people do. She stared straight ahead, trying to maintain her composure, shaking hands and hugging friends. She basically went through the motions, postponing the tidal wave of grief that would inevitably overtake her.

Marie was having an almost opposite reaction. She muffled her loud sobs with her handkerchief. She was unable to respond to handshakes or hugs. She was inconsolable.

John, Jr. was focusing on his mother — being strong for her sake. As I watched him put his arm around her shoulders, I knew he would have to work through his grief in his own time, in his own way.

Alice Evans sat and tried to exchange social niceties with everyone. It was clear, nonetheless, she was in a daze — that surreal feeling you get when your mind is overwhelmed by what is happening around you.

The funeral was complete, but the Evans family still had needs.

Members of my staff would be at the Evans home that afternoon, providing chairs for guests and a book for them to sign. I would be back at the cemetery later in the day to insure the burial vault was properly sealed.

And, I would call Alice Evans that night and the next day, just to check and see how she and her family were doing.

Having made the commitment to serve them to the best of my ability, by the end of the week, I would have put in more that 100 hours of work to serve the Evans family.

Family Discussion

1. How do you feel about cemeteries? Do you think of them in a negative way or in a positive way?

2. Have you ever taken a walk in a cemetery and read the inscriptions on the headstones? Describe.

3. What would you want to have engraved on your own headstone?

4. What would you like the officiant to say at your burial service?

5. Have you ever felt awkward about offering words of condolence at a graveside service? What are some other possible things you can say besides "I'm sorry"?

6. Should the funeral home's service to the family end with the burial? Why or why not?

"It will come back to you eventually," I said. *"Right now all you can so is just go through the motions. In time, it will get better. It really will."*

9

The Weeks After

One week later, I drove by the Evans house on my way to work.

Everything looked different from the way it appeared the afternoon of the funeral when cars filled the driveway and lined the street for an entire block.

Two members of my staff and I had spent hours there, supplying chairs from the funeral home for all the visitors and making sure they had the opportunity to sign the guest register. We kept watch and helped to maintain order while several hundred friends and well-wishers were in and out of the living room and front yard.

As I drove by and looked a week later, the house and street were quiet as if the crowds had never been there, as if nothing significant had happened.

It would have been easy for me to believe that nothing had happened. It would have been easy for me to dismiss the Evans funeral from my thoughts. After all, I had directed two additional funerals since then. I was once again functioning on very little sleep and had a visitation to coordinate in a matter of hours.

My responsibility to John Evans' family had ended with the completion of the burial and their payment of the bill, right?

Absolutely not.

I consider it unethical, unprofessional, and just plain insensitive to say to a family "Thanks for your business. Sorry about your loss. See you next time."

Anyone who has ever lost a family member or close friend knows very well that the hardest part of coping comes <u>after</u> the funeral.

~~~~~

During the visitation, funeral, and burial of a loved one, it is common for bereaved individuals to be suspended in a state of shock. They are carried along on the tide of all the arrangements, the social calls and the services.

When the last guest leaves and the last cousin packs up and catches a plane, however, the silence is overwhelming and the real grief begins.

~~~~~

My responsibility to Alive Evans and her children was to help them through the very difficult task of saying good-bye to John.

Saying good-bye is a <u>process</u>, not an event.

Their farewell to John would continue to be said in many different ways over a period of years, and I knew it was my duty to see them through, at least, the beginning of that process.

Impulsively, I dialed the Evans number on my car phone. I had originally planned to call Alice Evans later in the day when I was back at my office, but something said "Do it now".

"Alice?" I said, when she answered.

She recognized my voice before I had the chance to identify myself and began thanking me again for the funeral and graveside services.

"You're very welcome. I'm glad you were please," I replied.

This was almost the same conversation we had the day after the funeral when I called to check on her.

"How are you and your family doing?" I asked, tentatively, trying to stay on that thin line between what she would perceive as concern and what she might consider nosiness.

"Oh well...we're making do, you know. We're just sort of....," her voice trailed off.

An awkward silence followed.

"Alice, I know how difficult the first week after the funeral can be. I've been there myself." I began, hoping she would not cut the phone call short. "I've experienced it personally and I see it every day as part of my job. Don't expect things to go back to normal. Life won't feel 'normal' for a long time. No one expects you to pretend that it does."

At first she didn't respond and I wasn't sure if she was still on the line. Then I heard the muffled sound of a sob. Her voice broke as she answered me.

"It's just so...it's...I'm not even sure I can do this."

"Alice, would you like for me to stop by to see you? I'm on my car phone and I'm very near your house. Why don't I just come by to check on you for a few minutes? Would that be all right?"

She agreed. I drove around the block and back to her house. I was in danger of being late to the office but this visit was important to me, professionally as well as personally.

~ ~ ~ ~ ~

Just as a physician is concerned about the welfare of his patient during, as well as, after the hospital stay, a funeral director should be concerned for the families he or she serves for a long time afterward.

This is not an attitude or service unique to my funeral home. It is called 'aftercare' and it is becoming a routine part of most funeral homes' packages of services. Some funeral homes, as a matter of fact, employ a full-time grief counselor to help families for an indefinite period beyond the day of the funeral.

One may think that a bereaved family has no wish to see the funeral director again because they associate him or her with painful memories of the funeral. That's not generally true.

Alice Evans did not feel that way.

I rang the doorbell. The sound of it echoed through the house. The wooden door was designed in the old-fashioned style so common on houses built soon after World War II. At my eye level were three diagonal rectangular panes of glass. I tried to imagine the many times Alice and John had answered the doorbell, welcoming friends, colleagues, cub scouts, and grandchildren into their home.

I could almost hear their voices.

Alice opened the door. She was wearing the same green pantsuit she wore the day she and her family came to my office to plan the funeral. Her silver hair was pulled back, as if done in haste, by a terry cloth headband. The smile on her face looked almost painted on by her peach-colored lipstick.

"Please come in," she said graciously and a bit too formally as if trying to make up for her lapse of composure on the phone minutes before.

We sat down on the floral-print couch in the living room.

"John, Jr. will be over in a little while. He's taking me out to dinner," she said. "He has been my rock through all this, you know."

"I know he has," I replied. "I'm sure your husband would be very proud."

Alice's smile was natural this time.

"Yes, I know he would be. He and John, Jr. are so much alike, you know.

She paused.

"It makes it so much easier having him here in town."

Alice explained that her son came by every morning before work and had breakfast with her. Barbara phoned her every morning at ten o'clock. Marie called in the evenings just before bedtime.

"It helps us all just to talk every day," she said, clasping her hands in her lap. "I keep assuring them that I'm just fine, but truthfully, and I wouldn't tell the children this for the world,

I feel a lot like I'm just barely holding my head above water."

I knew this was true. It was true of my Aunt Jeanette when my Uncle James died. It would also be true for me when the time came for one of my own parents to pass away.

"I wake up in the morning, and the first thing I think of is John...out of habit, you know, and I catch myself wondering how he is doing at Rosewood, wondering whether he had a good night or a bad night. And then...it hits me...I remember that he isn't there. I remember that he isn't really anywhere that I can get to him and check to see how he's doing. Then I say to myself, 'Alice, get out of bed and get the coffee on.' But suddenly, I wonder...Why? Why do it? What's it for? What does any of it really matter?"

I nodded my head. This was a very common part of the early stages of grief.

"I look out the window at the cars driving by and I think, 'Where are they all going? What's the point of going any where? What is there to do?" Alice continued, mostly to herself. "Edna St. Vincent Millay wrote a poem I keep thinking about. It's in a book I got from the public library and never returned."

She looked at me sadly.

" 'Life must go on,' the last line says, 'I forget just why.' And that's exactly how I feel."

"It will come back to you eventually," I said. "Right now all you can so is just go through the motions. In time, it will get better. It really will."

"Do you think so?"

Her eyes looked directly into mine. She really wanted to know if this was true.

"I know so. But...you will grieve for a very long time. Allow yourself that."

I was giving advice from my own personal experience and not from any academic training in the field of counseling.

Some funeral directors prefer that a professional counselor give this type of service and I can see the wisdom in that. I also think, however, that a funeral director must be able to comfort people in their grief and must be willing to do it face to face.

Grief counseling conducted by funeral homes will soon become a standard. For those funeral homes that do not have a counselor on staff , usually there are books, audiotapes, and videotapes available for check out to help families cope with their loss.

I heard the back door open.

"Mom?"

John, Jr. had arrived.

"We're in the living room, hon'," Alice called out.

John rounded the corner and saw me sitting with his mother.

I stood up to shake his hand.

"I just stopped by to see how your mother is doing," I explained. "If there is anything at all I can do for her or for you, just name it."

"Thank you very much. We appreciate your concern," he answered politely.

"It's time for me to get back to the office, but I'll be calling again soon." I explained and walked towards the door. "I hope you have an enjoyable dinner."

With that, I was out the door and soon back in traffic on my way to prepare for a visitation. The image of Alice Evans sitting on the couch with her son standing at her side remained with me for the rest of the day.

This was not the last time I would sit with her in her living room on the floral couch and listen to her recite Edna St. Vincent Millay's poetry. I knew it wouldn't be.

Soon, I was to hear from the Evans family again, and this time it would be them paying me a surprise visit.

Family Discussion

1. Do you think it was proper for the funeral director to visit Alice Evans? Why or why not?

2. Have you ever experienced the feeling of uselessness as described by Alice Evans? How long was it before you began to feel "normal" again?

3. Which would be the more difficult part of a funeral director's job: handling arrangements or 'aftercare'? Explain your answer.

NOTES

"I've been thinking about this for a long time," Alice said resolutely, "and I know now what I want to do. I have heard that it's possible to make funeral arrangements in advance. If that's true, I definitely want to do it."

10

A Simple Plan

I have always liked autumn, from the changing colors of leaves to the winds blowing them from their branches and sending them spiraling down to the ground. There is something about the graceful changing of the seasons that appeals to me. The year is coming to its end. The design in the rhythm of that change is unmistakable.

In a way, I believe this is a reflection of how I feel about the cycle of life — birth, childhood, adulthood, old age, and death. Death is not an unnatural, horrific interruption of normality. It is, instead, part of the rhythm, part of the journey.

November is an especially beautiful time. I was staring contentedly out the window and watching the leaves when the telephone on my desk rang.

Lila, the office manager, told me I had visitors in the lobby. I reluctantly stood up and walked out to greet them. It was highly unusual for families in need of our services to stop in without an appointment, but I did have the next hour and a half free — plenty of time for an initial consultation.

The visitors met me halfway down the hall and to my surprise I saw Alice Evans and her son, John.

It had been more than six months since I had seen them last but I had not forgotten the Evans family. I knew from an article in the society section of the newspaper that Alice was active in one of the local garden clubs. I had also read in the business section about John, Jr.'s venture into owning his own business. He had resigned from his job as an insurance salesman and opened a sporting goods store.

"Alice, John. How are you?" I asked warmly, reaching out to shake hands with the both of them.

They each responded they were doing well. From the look in Alice's eyes, I believed her. I showed them into my office where we all sat down.

I wondered what had prompted the visit and hoped it was not any dissatisfaction with any of the funeral home's services last spring.

"I know you probably weren't expecting to see us in your office again so soon," John began, clasping his mother's hand. "And, to be honest, I didn't expect to be seeing you again for some time."

"God willing," Alice added. "We won't be here again for the same reason we were here last spring for a very long time."

I was happy to hear that no one in the family was critically ill or had died. Yet, I was intrigued by their visit. They both looked healthy, contented, and completely relaxed. I wondered how I could help.

"When my husband died," Alice said softly. "I was...we were not really prepared. He had been sick for many months and we all knew the outlook wasn't good, but still..."

"We just weren't ready for it. It was still quite a shock." John continued for her.

"There were so many things that caught us off guard. A lot of loose ends to be tied," she added.

I nodded my head as I recalled their ordeal.

"One of the biggest problems was his will. He didn't get a chance to update it the last several years before his death. So...as you can imagine, it didn't really reflect what he would have wanted and that ended up causing some real tension in the family...especially among the children." Alice said.

I was beginning to see where the conversation was going and how I could indeed help them. John confirmed what I guessed.

"Another problem was that we didn't know for certain what Dad's wishes were regarding his funeral and burial," he explained.

This was so true. The Evans family certainly experienced high levels of stress and tension because they did not know John, Sr.'s preferences. They had to guess and argue over what they individually felt was appropriate. The unpleasant scene had unfolded in this very office. While it wasn't the most hostile family argument I had ever seen, it certainly impaired their ability to support and uphold each other during such a traumatic time.

"I've been thinking about this for a long time," Alice said resolutely, "and I know now what I want to do. I have heard that it's possible to make funeral arrangements in advance. If that's true, I definitely want to do it."

I smiled.

"Not only is it possible, Alice, it is very easily done. And once the plans are taken care of, you can relax knowing your family will not have to agonize over what you might have wanted or what you would have forbidden them to do.

"Exactly." Alice answered and turned to John. "I don't want you and the girls getting angry at each other when I'm gone. I don't want any backbiting or any squabbling. It will help me immensely to know that you'll have each other to lean on."

~ ~ ~ ~ ~

What Alice was actually asking me to do was pre-arrange her funeral, much in the same way parents pre-arrange and begin to pre-pay for their children's college education.

Here is how the system works: Alice and I would sit down and do exactly what she and her children did for her deceased husband. She would decide what type for funeral she wanted, including the type of casket and type of burial.

The funeral home will typically have a printed worksheet, often in multiple choice questions and fill-in-the-blank format for the client to complete.

Pre-arrangement of funeral plans is good for the client psychologically. I believe it makes clients feel that although they cannot control how and when death will come, they can still take charge of the situation and choose how they want their death to be commemorated.

They are able to make plans and then go about their daily lives, their business in peace, knowing that should anything happen to end their lives, their wishes would be in writing and would be respected.

In Alice's case, she felt very strongly that she wanted an inexpensive to mid-priced casket with pale blue lining. Pre-arrangement allows one to be that specific or if preferred to just choose the basics and leave the details to the family.

Her son still had some questions about the practicality of advance arrangements.

"But what if Mom was to move to another city or state? Wouldn't she have wasted her time and money making these arrangements?"

I was glad to be able to tell him that none of her effort would be in vain if she moved out of town. Few people realize that it is possible to transfer such arrangements as well as the financial investment to another funeral home in another location. The original funeral home would not retain the account but allowing this kind of transfer is fair to the consumer.

Alice also had the freedom to plan her funeral and pay for part of it in advance or make the plans and have her family take care of the financial arrangements later. On this Alice wanted to relieve her children of as much financial obligation as possible and chose to pay for her funeral in advance.

"I don't have the money to pay for everything up front today," she confided. "Can I just pay in installments?"

I explained that not only was it possible for her to pay in installments, Alice had more alternatives than she realized.

First, she had the option of working with a local bank to set up an individual retirement account (IRA) that would pay the beneficiary — perhaps someone on staff at the funeral home — in the event of her death.

Another alternative for her was to purchase Forethought Insurance which is a special brand offered specifically for people pre-arranging funerals using caskets from the Batesville Casket Company. Since many funeral homes order caskets from this company, Forethought is a popular consumer choice.

Funerals can be arranged and paid for almost down to the last detail. I say 'almost' because there is one exception. It is not the policy of most funeral homes to allow advance payment for the actual opening and closing of the grave. The cost of this service changes so routinely it is not practical to freeze the price years in advance.

~ ~ ~ ~ ~ ~

After I answered all of their questions, Alice and her son were satisfied that she was making a wise decision to pre-arrange her funeral.

She selected a casket, the type of funeral she wanted, the type of burial plot she preferred, and a specific kind and size of headstone.

Alice did not write the funeral home a check for the full amount. Instead, we worked out a simple payment plan that would settle her bill in its entirety upon her death.

As I returned to my office after accompanying Alice and her son to the car, I had a deep sense of satisfaction knowing that my assistance had brought them full circle.

From the first moment that the telephone call advised me of John Evans, Sr.'s death up to the time I sat down with his widow and son to pre-arrange her own funeral, I had honored my personal commitment to conduct my practice as a funeral home director with compassion, good stewardship, efficiency, and integrity.

Family Discussion

1. What was your initial reaction when you first heard of the funeral pre-arrangement option? What is your opinion of the procedure now?

2. Has you perception of funeral directors changed after reading this book? Why or why not?

3. What is your comfort level with discussing the subject of death and funerals? Has reading this book helped to improve it?

I sincerely believe perceptions would change if people knew the depths of empathy, the commitment of reliability, and the significant amount of difficulty involved in helping families say good-bye to their loved ones.

Glossary

Aftercare - services provided by the funeral home to help families cope with grief.

Casket - an oblong box usually made of wood or metal to enclose the body of a deceased person.

Coffin - another word for "casket", used chiefly outside the United States.

Coroner - a county or city officer who investigates deaths by causes other than natural.

Cremate - the process by which the dead human body is reduced to inorganic bone.

Cremains - human remains that have been cremated.

Crematory - the place for the cremation of human remains.

Crypt - an underground vault or chamber used as a place for burial.

Death Certificate - a document certifying that a person is officially and legally deceased.

Disinterment - the removal of a body from its resting place.

Embalm - the thorough disinfection and process of preservation of a human body prior to burial.

Entombment - the placing of a body within the tomb.

Eulogy - a speech given at a funeral in honor of the deceased person.

Epitaph - an inscription on a tombstone or grave marker in recognition of the deceased person.

Funeral Director - a funeral service practitioner who arranges funerals and supervises all the preparations; including, but not limited to: embalming, hosting visitations, coordinating logistics, and supplying obituaries to newspapers.

Grave Liner - an outer container.

Hospice - an organization which cares for the terminally ill.

Inter - to place a body in a grave or tomb.

Lowering Device - a mechanism which lowers the casket into the vault.

Mausoleum - a monument, usually architecturally impressive in appearance, where multiple bodies are interred.

Memorial Marker - a marker placed at the head of the grave.

Memorial Gardens - another word for "cemetery". Memorial gardens typically have brass or stone memorial markers rather than upright tombstones. Sometimes they are located within larger cemeteries.

Mortician - another word for "funeral director".

Obituary - a death notice and short biography of a deceased person.

Officiant - a person who conducts the funeral or memorial service.

Pall - a cloth which is placed over the casket.

Pallbearer - a person who chosen by the family of the deceased to help carry the casket.

Plot - a space where someone is buried in a cemetery.

Pre-Arrangement - planning a funeral in advance.

Pre-Funding - paying for the majority of funeral expenses in advance.

Removal - obtaining and transporting the body of a person from the place of death.

Urn - a container which holds "cremains".

Vault - an outer burial container.

NOTES

NOTES